Shiva

Lord of the Dance

Shiva

Lord of the Dance

James H. Bae

MANDALA

San Rafael

MANDALA

PUBLISHING

17 Paul Drive
San Rafael, CA 94903
Tel: 415.883.4055
Orders: 800.688.2218
Website: www.mandala.org
E-mail: info@mandala.org

ISBN: 1-886069-95-6

Designed & Printed *by* Palace Press International

Printed in Hong Kong

Contents

Introduction

Om Namah Shivaya
'I offer my heart unto Shiva'

The Lord lives in the faces of all beings,
in their heads and in their necks.
He lives in the innermost heart of all,
the all-pervading, all-present Shiva.

—Shiva Purana

Introduction

Shiva, the Lord of the Dance, is a deity of ambiguity and paradox. He is both Shiva the terrible and Shiva the graceful. On one hand, he incarnates as death and time, lurking in the cremation grounds with a garland of skulls around his neck. He is surrounded by ghosts, evil spirits and demons, and is attended by malicious phantoms.

On the other hand, he is the greatest ascetic and patron of ascetics, the master of the yogis, meditating in the vastness of the Himalayas. The universe depends on the penances of Shiva. His austere performances harness the creative forces of nature prior to restoring the cosmos through his mystic dance. Shiva is also known as the destroyer, and in this role, as in his many other roles, he both terrifies and fascinates.

Among the many iconographic motifs that portray Shiva, he is best known as the yogi, the family man, the lingam and the Lord of the Dance. As the yogi, Shiva is commonly depicted sitting on a tiger skin in deep

meditation, high on the slopes of Mount Kailash. His third eye symbolizes both superior wisdom and insight. His body is smeared with ashes and his long matted hair tied in a topknot and decorated with a crescent moon. As the family man, Shiva is surrounded by his beautiful wife Parvati, their sons Ganesh and Skanda, and his mount, the bull Nandi. He is also worshipped in the form of his lingam, or phallus: detached from the world yet incarnating cosmic sexuality. This is the mystery of the "erotic ascetic," in whom there is no distinction between creation and liberation, *samsara* and *moksha*. And as Nataraj, the Lord of the Dance, Shiva rhythmically plays his drum, synthesizing the principles of both destruction and creation. In him, the finite and infinite meet, and all opposites are reconciled. ■

The Flow of Purity

One of Lord Shiva's names is Sthanu,
the immovable. Deep in meditation,
he sits as still and solid as a mountain.
A crescent moon rests on his crown
and a heavenly river cascades over
his matted locks. This is the tale of
how Shiva came to bear the Ganges
on his head.

Once, there was a king in Ayodhya

named Sagara, who had no heirs. He and his two wives retired to Kailash, Lord Shiva's abode in the Himalayas, to perform austerities. Their hope was to receive blessings for a child. In time, Shiva himself appeared to them and said to Sagara, "One of your wives will bear sixty thousand sons, all of who will meet with destruction. Your other wife will give birth to but one boy, whose descendents will bring glory to your dynasty."

When his sons had grown to adulthood, Sagara decided to sponsor the royal horse sacrifice to consolidate his influence throughout the kingdom. In accordance with this custom, a stallion was released to wander the empire.

Unless a competent warlord challenged the horse, the land it roamed through would become a part of Sagara's empire. Indra, the god of the heavens, was envious of Sagara, so he stole the sacrificial horse in order to thwart him. When the animal went missing, the king became worried and sent out his sixty thousand sons to find it. The princes searched everywhere, even digging deep into the earth, but to no avail.

One day, the princes heard the horse had been seen near the hermitage of the sage Kapila. Suspecting the sage of having stolen the beast, they interrupted his deep meditation and accused him of the theft. It is said that a false accusation directed at a holy

man dooms the accuser. In this case, fire spontaneously erupted from one and all. The flames quickly enveloped them and soon the sons were reduced to a pile of ashes.

Sagara had one surviving grandson, Amshuman, a descendent of his other wife. He followed the princes' route and found their ashes. Even so, he pleased Kapila by approaching him respectfully. The sage thus returned the horse, which permitted the successful completion of the king's sacrifice. He also told Amshuman that his relatives could only be redeemed if the sacred waters of the heavenly Ganges washed over their remains. Kapila gave a blessing to Amshuman that his grandson would be the one who brought the holy river into the world of mortals.

Many years later, Amshuman's own grandson, Bhagirath, sought to fulfill this prophecy and redeem his ancestors. He went into the Himalayas to perform penances and pray to Mother Ganga to descend to earth. Through Bhagirath's ardent endeavor, Mother Ganges finally agreed to descend from heaven, but she warned him, "When I come spilling down from heaven, my current will be so furious that unless something immovable is there to stop it, it will go right through the earth and into the netherworld. Only Shiva, the blue-throated

god, has the power to hold back my forceful torrent, so go to Kailash and appease him."

Bhagirath did as he was told and was rewarded by Shiva's reassurance that he would bear the cascading Ganges in his matted locks as she plummeted down from the sky. Soon Bhagirath was able to behold this marvelous sight. All the gods and sages, along with the heavenly singers and dancers, assembled there to watch the divine event with him. Ganga Devi fell frothing from the heavens, along with whirlpools, fish and crocodiles. She fell onto Lord Shiva's forehead like an endless garland of pearls. The spray looked like a flock of white swans circling around his head. The river broke into three separate braid-like tributaries and then rushed helter-skelter over his body and down the mountainside. Ganga Devi looked to the entire world like a mad woman dancing, dressed in garments made of her own spray and foam.

As she came roaring down to the earth, Ganga Devi stopped and asked Bhagirath to show her where to land. He led her down to the seashore, to Kapila's ashram, where she washed over his forefathers' ashes. The sixty thousand sons of Sagara arose in heavenly forms and went to the world of the gods. Ganga Devi filled the holes they had dug in search of the sacrifi-

cial horse, creating the ocean. In this way Lord Shiva made it possible for the purifying waters of the Ganges to descend into this world. ■

Love and Sacrifice

Long ago, when the world was still young, the creator god Brahma entrusted Daksha with the task of populating the universe. Civilized, affluent, and influential, the great progenitor Daksha was married to Prasuti, the daughter of Svayambhuva Manu, the father of all humankind. Daksha and Prasuti had twenty-four daughters, the last and

most beloved of whom was the magnificent goddess Sati.

When Sati was of marriageable age, Daksha held her *svayamvara* festival, the ancient custom whereby a prospective bride's suitors compete for her affections. Gods and princes came from far-off lands in the hope of winning her hand, for she was the most enchanting woman in the universe. Sati, however, held Shiva in her heart. Ever since she had been a little girl, she had wished for no other husband but him.

On that most auspicious day, however, Shiva was absent. Her proud father, considering him to be a wild man of the forests unfit for his lovely daughter, had snubbed Shiva by neglecting to send an invitation. Thus, when Sati came into the assembly of suitors, clutching the garland intended for her chosen groom, she was unable to find the one person she sought. Her heart filled with despair; Where was her beloved at this most crucial moment? Trembling, she threw the garland into the air and sent out a prayer to the great god. To everyone's surprise, Lord Shiva suddenly appeared out of nowhere in the midst of the crowd, with the garland adorning his neck.

Despite his daughter's evident love for him, Daksha continued to despise Shiva. Nevertheless, he was obliged to give him her hand. The other suitors were sent home disappointed,

and the divine couple was wed.

Though he enjoyed all the pleasures of worldly life, Daksha considered himself a religious and noble man. He was very fond of public sacrifices, which he performed with great pomp and circumstance. This made him feel important and respected. He was appreciated by his fellow citizens and lived a life of prosperity. In the end, however, this superficial happiness actually distanced him from what was truly meaningful in his life.

On one special occasion, Daksha held a sacrifice, to which he invited all the denizens of heaven. Lord Brahma was given the place of honor; Shiva sat to his right, and around them sat all the

major deities, sages and progenitors. When Daksha entered the arena, however, Shiva did not rise to greet him as would normally be expected of a son-in-law. Locked deep in meditation, Shiva was in fact showing respect to Daksha's soul, but the progenitor was too blinded by his own arrogance, wealth and influence to see it. He cursed the god and furiously made his exit, while Shiva remained seated, silent and stoic.

As the distance between Daksha and his son-in-law grew, Sati saw less and less of her sisters and their families. Nor would it have been possible to see them at will, living in the lonely Himalayas, as the couple did. One day, she heard that her father was planning the grandest sacrifice of all, and that all her family members were to be present there. Though neither she nor her husband had been invited, Sati decided to attend. Shiva warned her that she would only be met with indignity, but she was insistent. Shiva gave her his bull Nandi to carry her and sent his associates, the ghosts and goblins, to protect her from danger.

Upon her arrival, Sati was disheartened to see the extent to which her father had disowned her. Although the sacrificial site was glamorously ornamented with rare jewels, fine music and gorgeously dressed guests, it held no attraction for her. As she entered the arena, Daksha ignored her. While this pained her greatly, it was the lack of respect shown for her husband that wounded Sati more.

Daksha arose from his seat and began to condemn her and Lord Shiva in full view of the assembly. "All my daughters bring me joy, and their husbands respect," he bellowed. "All of them are greater than your Shiva. You alone bring me dishonor and fill me with disgust."

Daksha's harsh words brought tears to his daughter's eyes. She responded with a rebuke that pierced the skies: "Father! The Vedas themselves glorify my Lord and spouse, Shiva. Your disregard for him brings misfortune upon you. You will never

attain true happiness, no matter how many sacrifices you sponsor or perform. Your only hope is to receive the blessings of my husband, whose grace even great yogis aspire to obtain."

No longer able to bear Daksha's offenses to her beloved husband, Sati called upon her mystic powers and exploded into flames. The entire assembly looked on with horror as she was reduced to ashes before them.

When Shiva heard the news of Sati's demise, he collapsed into an ocean of grief and anger. His rage spawned a powerful demon, his destructive aspect, Virabhadra. Virabhadra mounted his chariot and, along with the countless hauntingly freakish creatures that crawled out from beneath his hair, sped off toward the sacrifice site. There he cornered Daksha and announced, "Shiva has sent me here to share the loss of our beloved Sati with you."

On that note, he raised his hand and let out a horrifying roar; then, along with his ghoulish companions, he proceeded to deface the sacrificial arena. Soon much of the site was up in flames. Virabhadra personally ensured that Daksha met his fate in the most brutal way possible, by severing his head from his body. No one who had witnessed Sati's self-immolation escaped Shiva's fury that day.

Without the sacrifice, however, the

gods would not be satisfied and creation would begin to dissipate. Fearing their own destruction, they approached Lord Brahma to ask Shiva to be merci-

ful. Together, the remaining gods went to Kailash to see Shiva, who lived up to his name, Ashutosh, which means "quickly pacified." At Brahma's request, Shiva agreed to resuscitate Daksha, which he did by replacing his severed head with that of the sacrificial goat .

Once revived, the penitent Daksha was able to complete the sacrifice and the cosmos was returned to a state of balance, though he had to bear the mark of his shame forever more. ∎

An Act of Love

With the loss of his eternal companion
Sati, Shiva took refuge again in the
mountains and resumed his prac-
tice of *tapasya*, meditating on the
fullness of his own being. Not long
thereafter, however, Sati was reborn
as Parvati, daughter of Himavan, the
god of the Himalayas.

When Shiva came there to perform

tapasya, Himavan welcomed him and offered his young daughter as a servant. Parvati picked flowers for his offerings, cleaned the altar, and brought him kusha grass and water for his ritual needs. In this way, she served Shiva daily, and the rays of moonlight from his hair relieved her of any weariness. Despite Parvati's unwavering devotion, Shiva remained aloof, rapt in deep meditation.

In the meantime, a demon named Taraka had become all-powerful in the universe. Having performed intense penances from early on in his life, Taraka had received a boon—no one would be able to match his prowess. Before long he had ousted Indra

from his throne as king of the heavens, instilling fear in the hearts of all the celestials.

The powerless devas approached Lord Brahma, asking him to stop the demon. But Brahma explained that only a child born of Shiva could defeat Taraka and restore the cosmic order. "Sati has been reborn again as Parvati. No one but she could bear his divine seed. We shall all be saved only if they have a child."

At this, Indra conceived a plan. He asked Kama, the god of love, to arouse passion in Shiva so that he would impregnate Parvati. Their offspring would become the celestial general that could defeat Taraka.

Kama set off into the mountains with his friend, Spring, who created a romantic ambience. The flowers bloomed, the birds sang and the bees hummed as they swarmed through groves of lotuses and lilies. The music of the celestial courtesans pervaded the atmosphere. Despite it all, Shiva's meditation remained unbroken, for there are no obstacles strong enough to disrupt the concentration of those who have become masters of themselves.

Parvati happened to be in Shiva's ashram, wearing flowers in her hair, her lips reddened by the juice of mountain berries. Kama, the god of the flower bow, seized the opportunity to fire off his arrow named Fascination, which successfully pierced Shiva's body. Shiva's steadiness was slighty diminished, like the sea disturbed by the rising moon, and he turned his three eyes toward Parvati's face. Through sheer strength and self-control, Shiva restrained his shaken senses. Wishing to find the reason his mind had become disturbed, Shiva gazed out in all directions and caught sight of Kama, poised to attack with his bow again.

Shiva was outraged at Kama's attempted manipulation. With a piercing ray of fire emanating from his third eye, he incinerated the God of Love. Having swiftly obliterated Kama, as easily as Indra's lightning bolt cracks a tree, Lord Shiva vanished.

The ploy of the gods had failed. Parvati, too, was left sad and frustrated, thinking her chance to have Shiva as her husband was lost forever. Then she turned her mind from all thoughts of the world and undertook severe austerities in order to appease Shiva. After many years, Shiva finally returned, disguised as an old Brahmin, to test

her resolve and devotion. He tried to dissuade her from her penances, even insulting himself in an effort to prove their futility. When all his efforts failed, he revealed himself and said, "From this moment, I am your slave. I have been purchased by your tapasya, O gracious goddess!"

Once married, Shiva and Parvati spent a thousand years on Mount Meru so absorbed in their lovemaking that it seemed like a single night. Even so, the joys of lovemaking did not quench their appetite, any more than all the floods of the ocean could extinguish the volcanic fires that blaze beneath it.

The love play of the divine ascetics sent out an alarming wave of vibrations; the inhabitants of all realms of the three worlds were plunged into a state of panic. The earth shook and the gods were greatly upset. To add to this, the unchallenged Taraka still held the world hostage. The gods felt very anxious at the delay in conceiving their war god and so approached Vishnu for help. Vishnu said, "Devise some means by which Lord Shiva's seed will fall on the ground, for if it enters Parvati's womb, the child born will not only destroy the demons, but will also take over the throne of heaven. This is what happens when two such powerful yogis procreate."

The gods sent Agni, the Fire God,

to carry out the task. Agni disguised himself as a pigeon, fearing of the consequences involved in interrupting the great god's lovemaking. Nonetheless, he ultimately suffered Parvati's curse for this disruption, but Agni was successful. Sensing the intruder, Shiva's concentration was broken and he spilled his seed onto a reed bed along the banks of the Ganges. The divine prince Skanda was miraculously born there. The child later became a mighty general of the celestial army, and led it triumphantly into battle against the evil demon Taraka. ■

The Nature of Desire

In South India, regional traditions often portray Shiva as the wandering mendicant known as Bhikshatana. The ancients spoke of how the great ascetic god wandered their very lands, and how the forests, trees, and mountains—being his real home—were so dear to him. Completely naked, Shiva looked as if he were intoxicated; his hair was matted and his skin smeared with dirt from the forest floor. Even so, this façade could hardly conceal his divine personality. Shiva's third eye was luminous with divine knowledge and his godly beauty shone through the dust and ashes that covered his body.

In this disguise, Shiva once entered the Pine Forest in order to teach a lesson to the many sages who lived there with their wives. On the one hand, he wanted to remind these sages that austerities alone are insufficient to obtain the ultimate release; on the other, he wanted to expose their hypocrisy, for though they externally observed asceticism, inwardly they were attached to their spouses in a way detrimental to their spiritual progress.

As Shiva made his way through the village, everyone was drawn to him, to his magic and his madness. Though he was a spectacle, no heart could shy away from him. He enchanted everyone in spite of their reservations, and even the chaste wives of the sages followed behind him. He smiled and hummed melodiously, setting the fire of passion aflame in their hearts. Their clothes loosened and slipped, in some cases revealing their trembling bodies. Some of the women hailed the great god, beseeching him seductively, "What is your name? Come and rest awhile. Your travels must have made you weary."

The advances of the sages' wives brought a smile to Shiva's face, but only astonishment and outrage to their husbands. They quickly gathered together to put a curse on the unknown visitor. They mustered their collective powers, achieved through austerities and the chastity of their wives, but it was all in vain. Finally, they fell upon Shiva with blows, accusing him of hypocrisy: "You are a false ascetic. You pretend to be renounced, but by showing yourself in your nakedness you cause our wives to become unfaithful to us. You should cut off your linga, for only when you are free from it will you be worshiped."

The great yogi said to them, "I will, if you hate my linga so." With that, he tore it off and vanished. The world suddenly turned dark and signs of doom and disaster began to manifest everywhere. Afraid, the sages went to see Lord Brahma and told him everything that had happened. Lord Brahma instructed them, "Being proud of your austerities, you failed to recognize Shiva. Because you were mentally attached to your wives, all your austerities were dry and superficial. You thus became angry with him. Now take shelter of Lord Shiva in the form of his linga, cultivate detachment in the company of your wives, and thus you will attain true wisdom."

Following Lord Brahma's advice, the sages fashioned an image of Lord Shiva in the form of the linga, as it is know today. They committed themselves to a life of spirituality, giving up the superficial physical chastity that had only caused the disease of lust to grow in their minds. By introducing the worship of the linga, Shiva showed that one must come to terms with desire, not by denying or attempting to conquer it, but rather by understanding its true nature. ■

Dance of the Divine Cosmos

"*Our Lord is the Dancer,* who, like the heat latent in firewood, diffuses his power in mind and matter and makes them dance in their turn."

—*Tiruvatavurur Puranam*

In the forest of Taragam dwelt a multitude of heretical rishis, or would-be holy men, who followed the path of ritual sacrifice through which they had obtained many magical powers. One day, Lord Shiva appeared there disguised as a naked renunciate to show them the futility of their actions. He was accompanied by the serpent god Ananta Shesh, and by Vishnu, who was disguised as a dazzling maiden named Mohini.

When the rishis of Taragam saw the three travelers, Mohini's beguiling body enchanted them. Their wives similarly lusted after Shiva. Before long, however, they realized their foolishness and became incensed at the undignified joke being played on them. They proceeded to light fires and perform a great sacrifice—which was the source of their magical power—offering oblations into the fire and muttering incantations.

With their first spell, a ferocious tiger, its jaws capable of tearing an

ordinary man in half, leapt out of the fire and charged Shiva. Shiva simply smiled gently and plucked the great beast out of the air as it lunged toward him. He stripped the beast of its skin with the nail of his little finger and wrapped it about himself like a silken cloth.

Undiscouraged by their failure, the sages renewed their oblations, this time producing a hideous serpent. They were filled with hope as they watched the venomous creature coil to strike Shiva, but the lord of yogis picked it up, hung it merrily around his neck like a flower garland, and began to dance wildly.

The rishis had not yet exhausted their black powers; they created one last monster in the shape of a malignant dwarf, Muyalaka. This time, however, the dancing Shiva pinned the hapless attacker down with his foot, breaking its back and leaving it writhing on the ground in pain. He then resumed his frenetic dance to the accompaniment of a band of celestial musicians, pacifying the minds of the rishis and mesmerizing the denizens of heaven who had gathered to watch the battle of mystic powers.

Surrounded by the gods and offset by the countless stars, Shiva could barely be distinguished from the dark night sky. The planets moved in concert with his limbs and the echoing pulse of his damaru drum revealed itself as the heartbeat of the cosmos. Streams of celestial waters cascaded down his matted locks and illuminated his glistening form, which gracefully swayed back and forth like waves washing on the shoreline on a full moon

night. Shiva was creating and defying all natural laws at once. His feet trod on empty space and his body engulfed the cosmos. His dance was a celebration of his fullness, an expression of the ecstasy of his blissful nature.

Beholding this mystic dance, Ananta Shesh glorified the great god and prayed to have this vision again. Shiva bestowed on him the boon of beholding this dance later in sacred Tillai, the center of the universe. Tillai, also known as Chidambaram, is the site of the Shiva Nataraj temple, where the four-armed form of the dancing Shiva has been worshiped for centuries as the Lord of the Dance. According to temple lore, Ananta Shesh

appeared there as the sage Patanjali, sometime in the early medieval period, to worship and serve this deity. Tillai also symbolically represents the human heart, where Shiva performs his blissful dance and destroys the bonds of ignorance.

Shiva Nataraj is one of the most potent sacred images to emerge from India. Every gesture expressed in his body is replete with deep philosophical import. In his outer right hand, he wields the damaru drum, symbolizing time and creation. In his outer left, he holds a flame that signifies his power of destruction. At every moment, as well as in periodic cycles, Shiva's creation dissipates and is again born anew.

His other right hand is raised in *abhaya mudra*, the gesture of fearlessness. As such, he encourages and empowers us to see beyond the veil of time and outward appearances. Shiva's expansive presence allows us to come to terms with the duality of this world. His lower left hand gestures toward his raised foot, symbolizing his bestowal of grace (*anugraha*). Trampling on the form of Muyalaka or Apasmara, the demon of forgetfulness, he eradicates the soul's ignorance.

Shiva's facial expression reveals a timeless serenity. He is emblematic of the space from which all things manifest, the underlying thread upon which each momentary event rests. His tranquil

gaze draws us into the center of silence where we remain ever aware of our being beyond the human predicament.

Nataraj Shiva's dance symbolizes five aspects of divine activity encompassing the entire cosmos: creation, conservation, destruction, incarnation and liberation. ∎

"Our Lord is the Dancer, In Tillai find our master Shiva's dancing form, His flitting foot, the tinkling sound of bells, The varying steps, the songs the celestials sing. Find them within, and all fetters will fall away."

—from Tirumular's *Tirumantram*

The Mystic Dancer

The dance of the Nataraj is not the only dance of Lord Shiva. There are at least two other forms. One is the gentle lyric dance (Lasya) of his benign side, which takes place at twilight on the heights of Kailash, accompanied by a divine chorus. Shiva places Parvati, the mother of the three worlds, upon a golden throne studded with precious

gems, and then dances while all the gods gather around him. Saraswati plays on the vina, Indra on the flute, while Brahma marks time on the cymbals. Vishnu beats the drum and his consort Lakshmi, the goddess of

fortune, leads the song. All the inhabitants of the three worlds assemble there to witness the celestial dance and hear the music of the divine choir.

The other dance of Shiva well represented in ancient iconography is called the Tandava. This fierce, violent dance belongs to his darker expression as Bhairava or Virabhadra. It is performed in cemeteries and cremation grounds where Shiva, usually in a ten-armed form, dances wildly with the Goddess, accompanied by troupes of capering imps. This dance precipitates havoc, and finally, the destruction of the universe.

"Here, the cremation ground symbolizes the aspirant's heart, where ignorance and karma are finally eradicated, and all notions of false ego disappear. At last the eternal soul finds its true nature through a direct encounter with Shiva." The perfect rhythm of this dynamic and triumphant joy is better expressed by dancing than by words. "He whom no sign can describe is made known to us by his mystic dance."

Nietzsche once said he would only believe in a god who could dance. Lord Shiva's dance is both an affirmation of life and a celebration of this world. At the same time, in the Tandava, it symbolizes the cosmic dance of time, in which he swallows all the ages and cycles of ages, but also exterminates the God of Death himself.

Life itself is characterized by duality, by teeming opposites. The myths of Shiva, however, ultimately point to a reconciling harmony that exists beyond our ordinary vision. By widening one's gaze to encompass life as a whole, life becomes a dance between extremes— a playful acceptance, an honoring, and a celebration. ■